THE FIRST BOOK OF

Snakes

REVISED EDITION

12 13 14 15

The author's thanks to Charles M. Bogert, A. M., Chairman and Curator, Department of Amphibians and Reptiles, The American Museum of Natural History, New York, for his helpful suggestions in regard to this book.

SBN 531-00631-x

Printed in the United States of America by The Garrison Corp.

THE FIRST BOOK OF
Snakes

BY JOHN HOKE

PICTURES BY PAUL WENCK

FRANKLIN WATTS, INC.
575 LEXINGTON AVENUE
NEW YORK 22, N. Y.

A SNAKE'S PLACE IN THE WORLD

Snakes have always seemed a little strange and mysterious to people—there's no doubt about that. Perhaps it's because of their peculiar shape, and their fascinating way of crawling. Or maybe it's because they're so silent. They slip quickly and quietly across our paths. They have no call, like most birds, or no howl, like many wild animals. Or it may be because they are so very alone and independent. Each snake lives completely on its own from the time it's a day-old baby. It never makes a home in which it raises a family, as many birds and animals do. And of course, some snakes are poisonous, and that makes people a little shy of them all, even the harmless ones.

As we find out more and more about snakes, we are realizing that there is nothing really mysterious about them. They have their own very special ways of living, just as any other animal does. And they have a very important place in the animal world. Most snakes are not harmful, many of them are valuable, and all of them are interesting. We know now what the ancient Egyptians probably understood when they started protecting snakes in their temples—many snakes are especially useful to the farmer. They eat a great many rats, mice, gophers, and other small animals that destroy the farmer's crops. Others eat snails, slugs and insects. And still others that are harmless themselves eat poisonous snakes.

Some people kill snakes without stopping to think. Often they kill valuable ones. Or else they kill snakes that are harmless, so should be allowed to live, valuable or not. If these people knew more about snakes, they would understand how wrong it is to kill one, just from senseless fear.

Corn snake

HOW SNAKES CAME TO BE

Snakes belong to a class of animals called reptiles. The only other reptiles alive today are crocodiles, alligators, turtles, tortoises, lizards, and one strange New Zealand creature called a "sphenodon," or "tuatara."

But for a long time, millions and millions of years ago, reptiles were the most important animals on the earth. They grew in many sizes and shapes. This was before there were any people, and before any of the animals that we know today developed. Everything was different—even the weather. It was very warm. Everywhere there were great swamps and jungles, full of giant ferns as big as trees.

The reptiles of those days were not like any that we ever saw alive. They were very odd-looking. And some of them were enormous, probably weighing more than twenty tons. Giant dinosaurs reared on their powerful hind legs. Winged reptiles called pterosaurs swooped through the air. Icthyosaurs, plesiosaurs, and, later, mososaurs lived in the water.

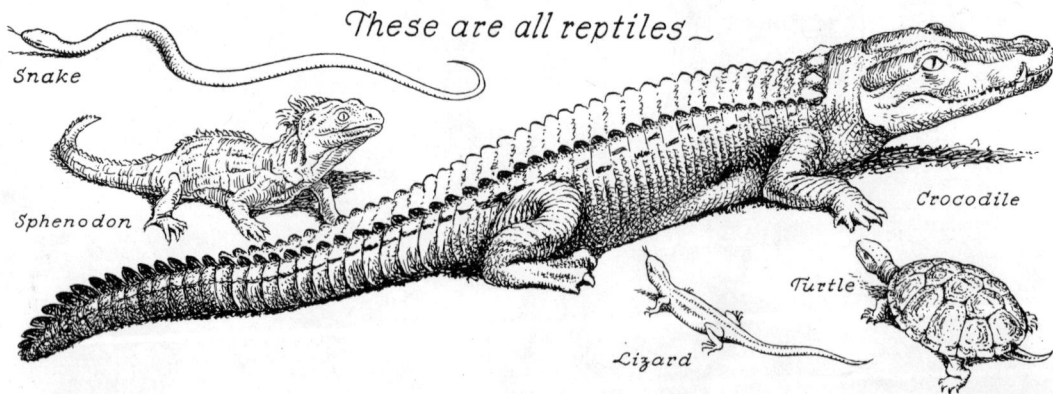

These are all reptiles

Snake

Sphenodon

Crocodile

Turtle

Lizard

Brontosaurus

Dinosaurus

Triceratops

There were many small reptiles, too. And as time went on, some of these small reptiles began to change, very, very slowly. They didn't change because they figured out that they would be better off if their bodies were different. In fact, things happened just the other way round. Take snakes, for instance. They came from a kind of lizard. These lizards started out with legs. But scientists think they lived either underground or in high grass. Anyway, their legs were a nuisance to them—always in the way. As time went on, some lizards were born with legs a tiny bit smaller. These new creatures got around faster; their enemies couldn't catch them as easily. As the years went by, their young kept changing more and more. They were able to get along better, so they survived. Finally after millions of years, they had changed so much that they became a new kind of reptile: snakes.

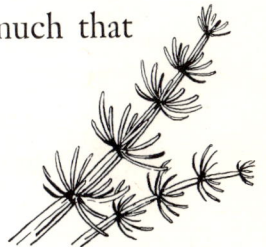

9

DON'T TREAD ON ME

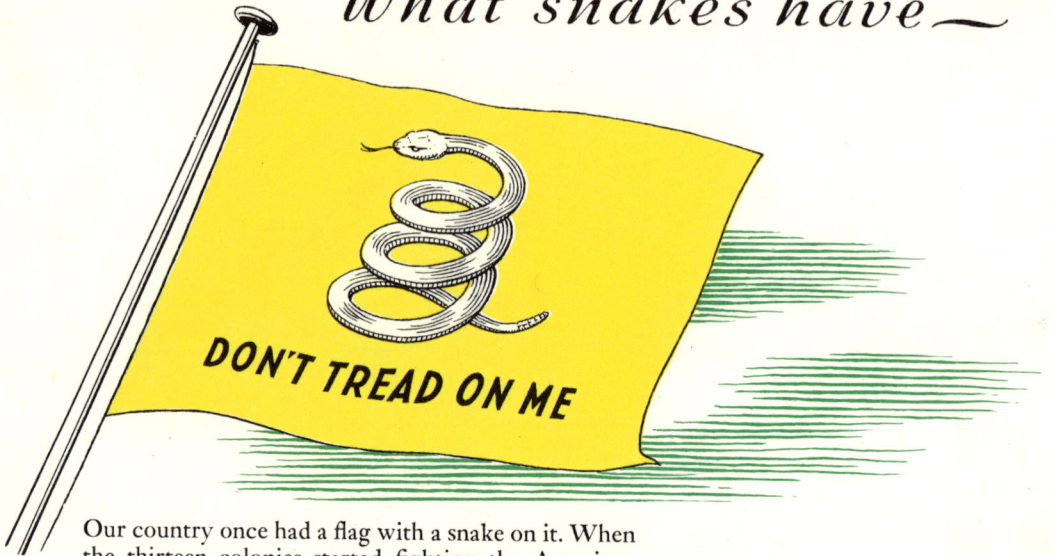

Our country once had a flag with a snake on it. When the thirteen colonies started fighting the American Revolution, they had no special flag. Someone thought of a banner showing a coiled rattlesnake with thirteen rattles, one for each colony. Underneath the snake were the words "Don't tread on me." This flag was used often before we had our official Stars and Stripes.

The ancient Pharaohs of Egypt attached a likeness of the royal serpent, an asp, to the front of their headdresses as a badge of their high position, as a protection from harm, and as a sign that they had the power to strike and destroy their enemies. This snake also showed that they claimed the sun as their ancestor.

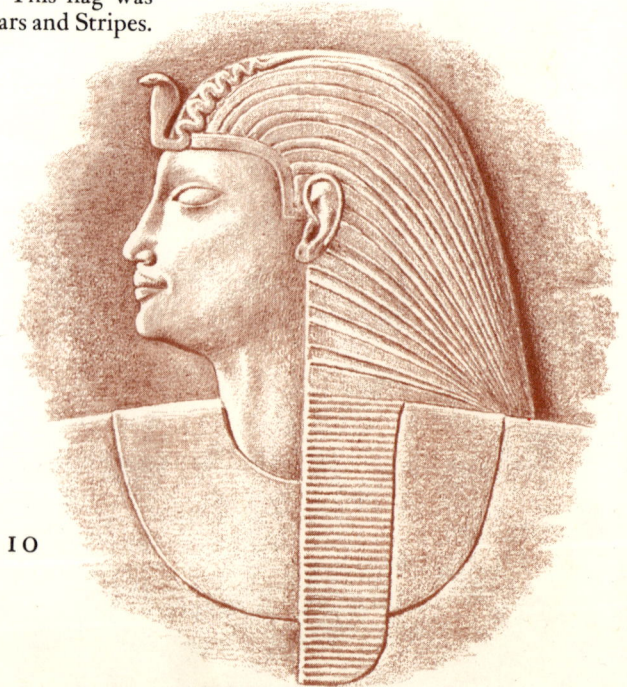

10

meant to many people.

Some early people believed that the earth rested on
three platforms. The lowest was a great snake coiled
in water. A giant tortoise stood on the snake's back.
On the tortoise's back were four elephants. And the
elephants held up that all-important platform, the
earth itself.

The early Egyptians believed that snakes were sacred, and thought them a sign of good luck. The people protected snakes and fed them in their temples.

Ancient people did not know the scientific reasons for many things. Some thought that earthquakes were caused by great snakes stirring around underground.

think about snakes.

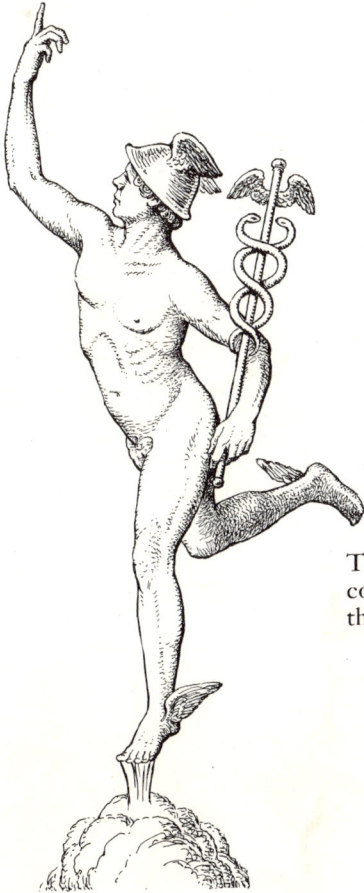

The ancient Egyptians and people of some other countries believed that the earth grew from an egg that was hatched by a huge snake.

The ancient Greeks thought snakes had healing powers and were a sign of wisdom and long life. Statues of Athena, Goddess of Wisdom, often had a snake on them. The Greek and Roman Gods of Medicine were often pictured holding a staff with a snake coiled around it. Mercury, messenger of the gods, was also shown carrying a winged staff with two snakes coiled around it. This is called a "caduceus," (pronounced ka-dú-se-us), from the Greek word meaning "a herald's wand," and is the insignia of the Medical Corps, U. S. Army.

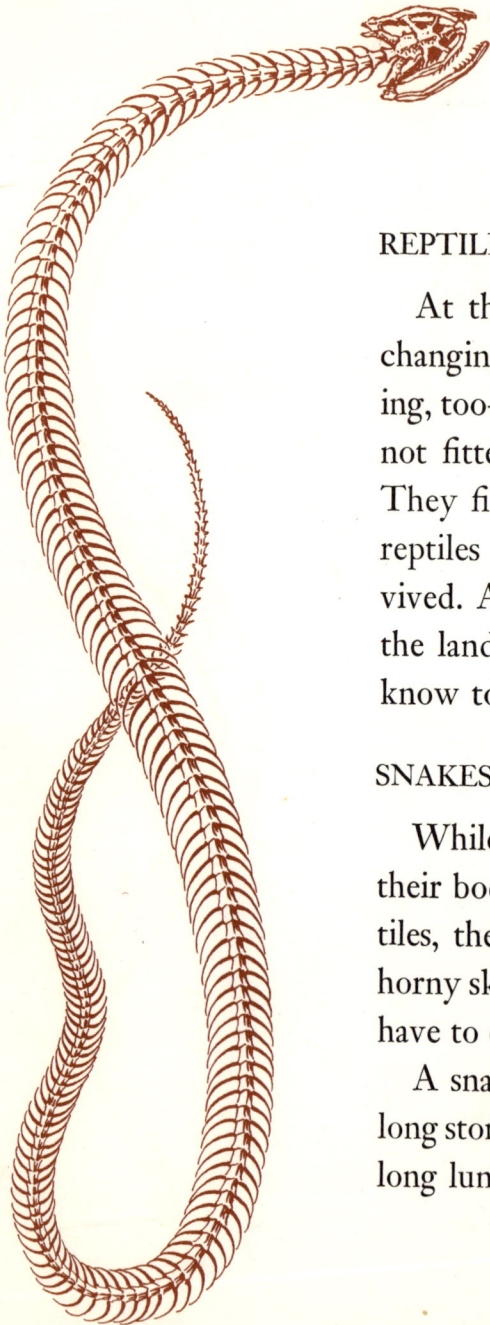

REPTILES UP-TO-DATE

At the same time that some reptiles were changing, the weather of the world was changing, too—becoming cooler. Giant reptiles were not fitted to live under the new conditions. They finally died out. But some of the small reptiles that had changed to new forms survived. And gradually, over millions of years, the land and air and some water animals we know today developed from them.

SNAKES ARE SPECIALLY BUILT

While snakes were developing without legs, their bodies were changing, too. Like all reptiles, they have scales—little plates of tough, horny skin—good protection for snakes, which have to crawl over rough ground.

A snake's body is long and slender, with a long stomach, a long heart, and usually just one long lung, to fit its streamlined design. Many

small bones joined together make up the backbone, which can bend at each joint. Some
snakes have over three hundred of these little
bones, so it is no wonder that they can coil
themselves up like flexible springs, as they so
often do.

"WALKING," A SNAKE'S WAY

From the backbone, a snake's ribs curve
down in pairs, so that a snake flat on the ground
is really resting on the ends of its ribs. These
are the snake's bony framework. On the
under side of a snake's body is a row of
strong, overlapping plates, one for each pair
of ribs. The front end of each plate is fastened by muscles to a pair of ribs. The rear
ends of the plates are not fastened at all. The
ribs are joined loosely to the backbone. And
many strong muscles join the ribs to each
other. Plates and muscles working together
can make a snake crawl along the ground.

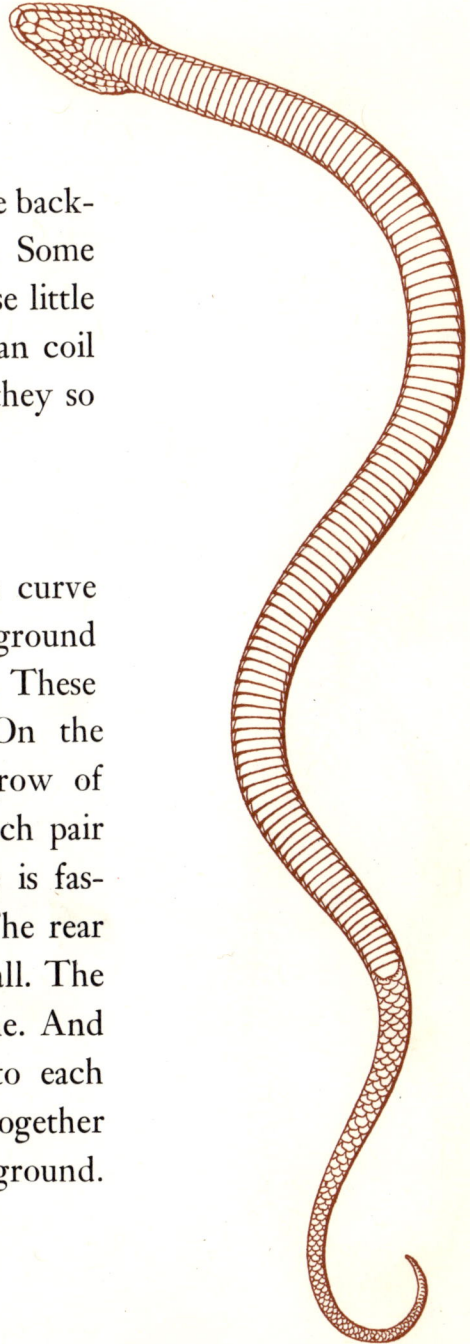

15

When a snake wants to move, it pushes its plates forward, a few at a time, starting from the front. Then it starts pulling them backward. But the loose rear ends of the plates catch on rough places on the ground. These rough places keep the plates from sliding back to where they were. And with the help of its strong muscles the snake hoists itself on top of these plates. This makes it go forward. It is a slow way to crawl. Heavy snakes often use it for hitching themselves along. They leave a straight track, as if a heavy piece of rope had been dragged along.

But snakes can crawl very fast in another way. They use their plates and muscles, and twist their bodies from side to side in little curves as they go along. Each curve follows in the path of the one before it. A snake can really zip along in this way because each time it bends its body it also gives a strong forward push against the rough ground. In soft earth, a winding track shows. Sometimes you can see little pushed-up piles of dirt on the curves, where the snake shoved itself forward.

Some snakes live in deserts where there is nothing but smooth sand, too slippery to push against. So some of the desert snakes have developed another way of moving, called "sidewinding." Sidewinding is a sort of rolling motion. The snake brings its head forward through the air. Then it curves its neck and rests it on the earth. At the same time, the snake's body rolls out at an angle to one side of the head, in an S-shaped path. So the snake goes *forward*, with a *sidewise*, rolling motion, leaving a peculiar, S-shaped track.

Snake experts can often tell what snake made a track, just by its looks.

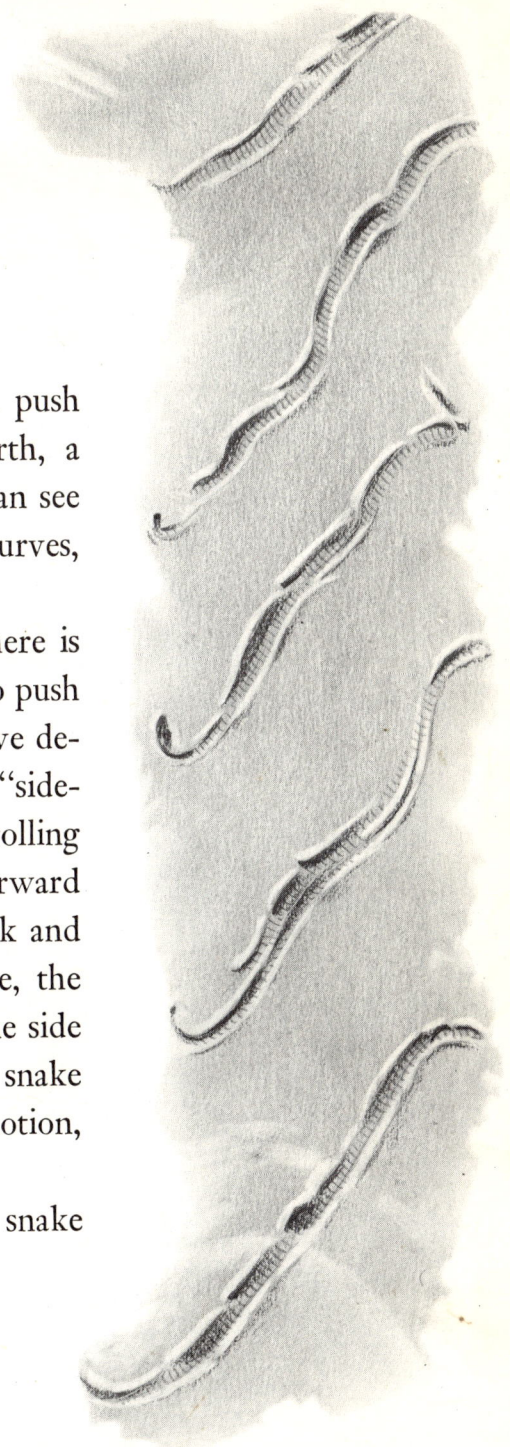

FINDING THEIR WAY

A snake has good eyes that see sharply, but for short distances only. Even its eyes are different from those of other animals. A snake has a transparent scale like a window over each eye, to keep out dust and dirt. This is really an eyelid, but immovable. So a snake never winks. It always looks as if it were staring. It even sleeps with its eyes open.

A snake has no paws, so it can't feel its way. It doesn't have whiskers to use as feelers, as panthers and cats and lions do. A snake's ears are not like those of many animals, and it cannot hear things in its path, in the ordinary way. All of this makes you wonder how snakes get along so well. Why aren't they always blundering into danger?

A snake's body helps, for it can feel vibrations along the ground. Besides that, a snake has something that makes up for its lack of ordinary equipment. If you have watched a snake, you have seen it flick its thin, forked tongue in and out of its mouth rapidly. This quick, sensitive tongue is the snake's own special tool for telling where it is going.

As the snake crawls, it keeps touching its tongue lightly to the ground. The forked tip licks up tiny particles and puts them in a place in the mouth where there is a sort of smeller. The tongue is very delicate. When it is not in use, the snake pulls it into a skin sheath on the floor of its mouth, to protect it.

WHAT A SNAKE EATS

All snakes eat animal food, and they often swallow it alive. Lizards, salamanders, frogs, tadpoles, birds, fishes, earthworms, insects, eggs, other snakes, a variety of small animals such as mice, gophers, rabbits, rats—all these are food for snakes. And some snakes can eat quite large animals, too.

What a snake eats depends on its size and on where it lives. Some tiny snakes that live underground eat ants' larvae. Some of the huge jungle snakes can swallow a small deer or a wild pig. Watersnakes live on fishes, salamanders, frogs, crayfish and other water animals. Some snakes like only a few kinds of things. And other snakes eat a great variety of food.

CATCHING FOOD

Because snakes have no paws, they have to be quick and tricky about catching food. Some can track down animals by smelling and others use their eyes to spot their prey. They slip along very quietly, following it, or else they lie perfectly still until an animal comes by. While waiting for food, a snake keeps its body in loose coils. When the animal comes close enough, the snake straightens out the front part of its body quick as a flash and grabs with its teeth. This is called "striking." A snake usually strikes quite quickly, and its aim is very accurate.

Some snakes catch food just by striking, getting it firmly between their teeth. But others make doubly sure of holding onto a good meal by using other tricks, too.

Some put a coil of their bodies over their victim to hold it down while they get ready to eat.

Some get a good grip on the animal, then like a flash they wrap themselves around it several times very tightly, and start squeezing. The more the animal struggles, the harder they squeeze, until finally it cannot breathe any longer. Then they loosen their coils and start eating. Snakes that wind around their food in this way are called "constrictors," and their squeezing is called "constricting."

And some snakes have another way of killing their food. They use poison, called "venom," which they make in glands in their heads. Little canals carry the poison from the glands to their fangs. Poisonous snakes' fangs developed from what were only enlarged teeth at first. Gradually, over thousands of years, these fangs became longer than teeth. Now they are very skillful mechanisms. The instant the fangs bite into a victim, the muscles of the poison glands give a quick squeeze, and out squirts the venom to make the animal helpless.

Some snakes have fangs at the back of their mouths, with little grooves on their surface down which the poison flows. These are the rear-fanged snakes. They have to force an animal back into their mouths with their teeth before they can poison it. Rear-fanged snakes in this country do not have enough poison to harm people.

Other snakes have their fangs in the front of their mouths. These fangs are hollow, with a hole near the tip, out of which the poison comes. They are really very much like the hypodermic needles you may have seen in a doctor's office.

One family of snakes, called "vipers," have fangs that are so long they have to fold back when not in use. They grow on movable bones. When the viper's mouth is closed, the bones pull the fangs back against its roof under folds of skin. Then, when the viper's mouth opens, the bones can be tilted, bringing the fangs down into position, ready on the instant.

22

lump

EATING, A SNAKE'S WAY

Snakes may differ somewhat in the ways they catch their food —some by grabbing, some by constricting, some by poisoning. But they all eat in the same way, a strange one, too. All snakes swallow their food whole. They never tear it apart first. And they never chew it, as many animals do, although their teeth do help them to swallow their food.

Sometimes snakes eat animals bigger around than they are. Garter snakes, which are small, can swallow quite large frogs. And a small snake can swallow a hen's egg about twice the size of its head. (Imagine—that is like a person swallowing a basketball!) It seems strange that snakes can do this, but again, the answer is that they have slowly become fitted for the lives they lead.

MOUTHS THAT STRETCH

Snakes have mouths that help them swallow big pieces of food. A snake's mouth is very large; it reaches way back toward the rear of its head. The upper and lower jaws are very loosely connected at the back of the mouth. A snake can drop its lower jaw far down, making a big opening into its throat. Its lower jaw is not in one piece, but is made of two curved pieces of bone, one on either side of the mouth. While a snake can move each part separately, these parts are joined by an elastic ligament. This stretchable ligament is very useful. It makes it possible for a snake to spread its lower jawbones way out to either side. So a snake can make room for animals much larger around than itself.

A snake's teeth are specially shaped to help, too. There is a row of them in each part of the jaws, and many snakes have a double row in each part of the top jaw. The teeth are all sharp as needles, but do not carry poison—only grooved or hollow fangs carry poison. Instead of growing straight up and down, these teeth curve back toward the throat. So, once an animal is in a snake's mouth, the more it tries to get out, the tighter it gets caught by the teeth.

Both teeth and fangs break quite easily, but new ones grow to take their places.

EATING TAKES TIME

A snake usually starts swallowing its prey head first. An animal goes down easier this way, especially if it has fur or feathers. Also, snakes that strike and seize an animal without killing it soon suffocate it by swallowing it head first. In swallowing, the snake grasps the animal between the teeth *on one side* of its jaws and anchors it with the sharp points, while it moves the other side of its jaws farther up over the animal. Then it anchors the teeth on that side and moves forward again with the first side, and so on, taking turns on either side. What it is really doing is crawling slowly up over its food with the help of its teeth and jaws.

Snakes have very elastic skin between their closely fitting scales. And when a snake starts to swallow something quite big, the skin between the scales starts stretching. Sometime you may see a snake eating, with its scales stretched far apart and the skin between showing—often a different color.

Sometimes, if the food is very large, a snake may take an hour or longer to finish swallowing it. In the meanwhile, the snake looks very uncomfortable, all stretched out of shape. And it has to stop now and then to rest its jaws. With its mouth crammed full, you might think the snake would have trouble in breathing. But not at all! It can push the front end of its windpipe forward, between the food and the lower jaw, and take in some air while it is resting.

MORE ABOUT EATING

Once the food gets past its teeth, and down as far as a snake's throat, the strong body muscles take over. They start working the food slowly down toward the stomach, much as your hands would work a table tennis ball down the inside of a long narrow balloon.

26

A snake's stomach has very strong digestive juices. They can digest bones and teeth and eggshells, and everything but such tough parts as feathers and claws. Eating a big meal stretches a snake so out of shape that you can see a great lump until its food is quite well digested.

A snake doesn't eat every day. After it has had a very big meal it may not eat again for a week or even longer. And some snakes can go without food for months, if they have to. But some snakes do have to have a good deal of water. They drink by sucking with their throat muscles. You can see the sides of their jaws go in and out as they take in water.

A few snakes have become experts at eating one kind of food. The egg-eating snake of Africa eats only eggs. The ends of some of its spinal bones grow into its throat, to make an egg-crusher which breaks the eggshells open. Then the snake eats the insides and spits out the shells.

SNAKES AND WINTER

Most hairy animals, as well as birds, have body temperatures regulated to stay always about the same, if the animals are healthy. They are "warm-blooded." But snakes are "cold-blooded." That means their temperature is unregulated by an inner mechanism. It depends on the temperature of their surroundings, and changes with them. Snakes cannot endure strong summer sun. If they stay in it too long they may die. They cannot stand freezing weather, for they will freeze to death. When fall comes, they start looking for a warm place to spend the winter, or to "hibernate," as it is called. Usually they go underground, for the ground holds some heat, even in winter.

Cracks that go deep into rocky ledges are favorite places for hibernating. Some snakes spend the winter alone. But often many snakes of different kinds—blacksnakes, copperheads, and rattlesnakes, perhaps—will all spend the winter peaceably together in one of these "dens."

Old woodchuck holes or other animal burrows, hollow places under trees, crevices in rocks, even crevices in the sides of wells, above the water line, are used by snakes as winter quarters. Hibernating is something like going into a deep sleep. The snakes lie quiet in their dens through the winter months, without even eating.

WHEN SPRING COMES

As spring comes on and they feel the warmth, snakes crawl out into the sun on warm days, going back into their dens at night. Finally, when warm weather is here to stay, they come out for good, and often start looking for food and water. About a month later, in northern climates, the mating season begins for most snakes, though some mate in the fall.

For mating, the male snake finds a female of his own kind, probably by her smell. Then, like most animals, he courts her. Each kind of snake seems to have its own kind of courtship. Scientists do not know very much about how some snakes court. They do know that male garter snakes and water snakes court by rubbing their chins along the backs of females. But there is much yet to be learned about the courtship of snakes.

By the end of May, in this country, mating is usually finished. Then the snakes all go their separate ways, to roam by themselves for the summer. Snakes do not live as families, and the mothers and fathers do not raise their young together, as many birds and animals do. Snakes live by themselves except during mating and hibernation.

BABY SNAKES

Snakes have their young in two different ways: some kinds lay eggs; and others give birth to little live snakes.

Live snakes are born in late summer or early fall. They come out through a little slit on the under side of the mother's body. Each little snake is in a clear thick sac that looks a little like wet paper. The baby snake soon breaks out of this. The number of young in a brood depends on the kind of snake. Some rattlesnakes have only four young snakes, and garter snakes sometimes have as many as seventy young in one brood.

Mother snakes that lay eggs begin to hunt for a good nest in June or July in this country. They like a place that is hidden and quite warm and just damp enough. The warmth and dampness help the eggs to hatch. Holes in rotting logs or sunny sandbanks, hollows in sawdust or leaf mold—all are good.

When the mother snake has chosen a spot, she lays her eggs, which are longish, with shells that are tough and leathery, not brittle like hens' eggs. The nestful is called a "clutch" of eggs.

31

Most mother snakes leave their eggs to hatch by themselves, and take no more interest in them. But some snakes guard their nests. And a few kinds sometimes coil around the eggs—although they probably cannot warm them enough to help much in hatching.

The number of eggs varies. A tiny worm snake may lay two eggs, a corn snake, one or two dozen in a clutch.

As they take in moisture from the nesting place, and as the little snakes inside begin to develop, the eggs actually grow larger! Even a snake's eggs are stretchable. And as they get ready to hatch they become lumpy and out of shape. Finally the young snakes are ready to come out. Some hatch in about two months from the time the eggs are laid. Others take longer, possibly almost three months.

Baby snakes hatched from eggs have a special little growth called an egg tooth on the very front of their heads, just above their mouths. They use this like a knife, to make slits in their shells. Then they sit with their heads sticking out, looking at the world. They do not hurry, but often take almost a day to come out of their shells.

From the moment they are hatched or born, baby snakes are independent—living their own lives. The mother snake never takes care of them. Baby snakes catch their own food and defend themselves, and a baby poisonous snake even uses its poison fangs as a grown-up one does.

A CHANGE OF SKIN

Snakes have a thin, almost transparent skin over their scales and eyes. After a few days, baby snakes shed this outside coating, along with their egg tooth (if they have one) and come out with a new skin that has been growing underneath.

Every so often, all their lives, snakes shed their topmost layer of skin. Many people think they do this because their old skin has become too tight and does not allow room for them to grow. But scientists say this is not so. Snakes shed their skin at intervals, even when they are not growing much.

For a while, before a snake sheds, its colors are very dull, the covering over its eyes is smoky white, and it cannot see much.

This goes on for several days, then the snake's eyes become clear, and its colors are brighter. Soon the snake starts rubbing its jaws hard against a rough piece of stone or wood. This breaks the old skin around its mouth. Then by rubbing against something rough, the snake rolls its skin backward toward its tail, wrong-side out, much as one peels a banana, except that the snake keeps its skin all in one neat piece.

Sometime you may find one of these old skins in a field or wood. They show exactly what the snake's body was like. There is a hole where the jaws were, and another hole for the slit on the snake's underside where it gets rid of waste material from its body. And there are marks like little lenses for each scale, and even for the two eye windows. Around these smooth scale marks is a rough network of the elastic skin that grew between the scales.

Right after shedding, snakes are particularly bright and shining, and their colors are at their most brilliant.

SNAKES' ENEMIES

Many people are afraid of snakes. But, in this country, snakes bite only in defense—when surprised or annoyed or frightened. Our only really harmful snakes are the poisonous kinds, which you will read about later in this book.

Among snakes' enemies, besides people, are hawks, owls, weasels, eagles, rats, hedgehogs, mongooses, and some other snakes.

If it has no fangs, a snake's best protection against its enemies is running away, slithering over the ground. Hiding, sometimes just by lying still, is protection, too. Snakes' scales are colored in many patterns which often match their surroundings. Many green tree snakes, lying quiet, look like leaves or growing vines. The copper and brown shades of copperhead snakes blend in with the colors of the forest floor. Some snakes fight, by constricting or biting. Some bluff, puffing themselves up and hissing, or doing other things. And poisonous snakes have their fangs as good weapons.

Hiding, fighting, running away, bluffing—a snake protects itself from enemies in all these ways. Many snakes merely lie still when danger threatens. Their scales are often colored to match their surroundings, and act as camouflage. Some snakes roll themselves into balls, with their heads in the center, when they are frightened.

Some snakes make loud hissing sounds, and strike with their heads, trying to frighten their enemies. A few kinds have a little flap of skin in front of their windpipes. When they let air out, it hits this flap, making their hiss sound especially loud. Often a snake's noise and threatening appearance are merely bluff. A harmless snake can put on quite an act.

fight their enemies

Some snakes frighten enemies by vibrating their tails. When doing this, they can make a great racket in dry leaves. A few snakes hide their heads from harm and shake their tails as if they were heads.

Some snakes can move the ribs of the front part of their bodies forward, and flatten them out so that their heads and necks spread into what looks like a hood. Several kinds of snakes do this, but cobras are the most famous for stretching out their hoods when they are in danger. They are poisonous, and live in Africa, Asia, and the Philippine Islands.

WATCH OUT FOR THESE

The only dangerously poisonous snakes in this country are rattlesnakes, water moccasins, copperheads and coral snakes. The first three of these belong to a family called "pit vipers." Like all vipers, they have fangs that fold back against the roofs of their mouths. They are called "pit vipers" because they have two little holes called "pits" on their snouts, about halfway between their eyes and nostrils, and a little below them. These pits have very sensitive nerves that can feel heat, even the heat of animals, a short distance away. Feeling this heat helps the pit vipers to aim their strike accurately.

The other kind of poisonous snake in this country, the coral snake, is not a viper. Its fangs are rigidly attached to its upper jaw and do not fold back.

Rattlesnakes, copperheads and water moccasins bear live young snakes. Coral snakes lay eggs.

The four kinds of copperheads range from New England to Florida and westward to Texas and Kansas. They are handsome, with coppery red heads, pale brown scales, and chestnut brown, hourglass-shaped bands across their backs. Copperheads usually do not grow over three feet long. They live most often in rocky, woody places, but they sometimes stray down into damp meadows, too. They eat mice, birds, frogs, lizards, insects and other snakes.

In copperhead country, be careful not to reach down and roll logs and stones with your bare hands. A copperhead might greet you most unpleasantly. Use a stick for moving logs and rocks.

Water moccasins live in the South Atlantic and Gulf States and up the Mississippi River valley as far as Illinois. They grow from three and one-half to nearly six feet long, and are a darkish brown or almost black when fully grown. Young moccasins are reddish brown with darker markings; they look a little like copperheads. Moccasins like the water and always live around it. They eat fish and frogs mostly, but also like birds, marsh rabbits, young musk-rats or other small animals. Moccasins stretch along branches over the water and sun themselves. They often stand their ground against enemies. Then they throw back their heads and open their mouths, showing the white lining. That is why many people call them "cottonmouths" or "gappers."

If you are in moccasin country, be wise and take no chances. Learn to know what they look like.

The coral snake, which is a relative of the cobras of Asia and Africa, is one of our most poisonous snakes. But you are much less likely to see a coral snake than any of the other poisonous ones. It is a burrowing snake and spends much of its time underground. And it lives only in the Southern states from North Carolina to Florida and to the lower Mississippi valley. In some ways, there is less danger from a coral snake than from pit vipers. Its fangs are shorter, so they usually do not strike through ordinary clothing, as a pit viper's often do. Coral snakes eat lizards and other snakes. They are round snakes with round heads, and they have red, black and yellow rings going all around their bodies.

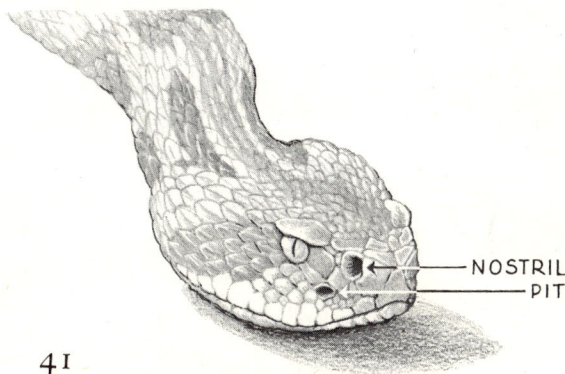

NOSTRIL
PIT

Probably our best-known rattler, living in the hot, dry South-west. Grayish, with darker diamonds edged with white, and with black and white rings on its tail. Grows to be about four and one-half feet long.

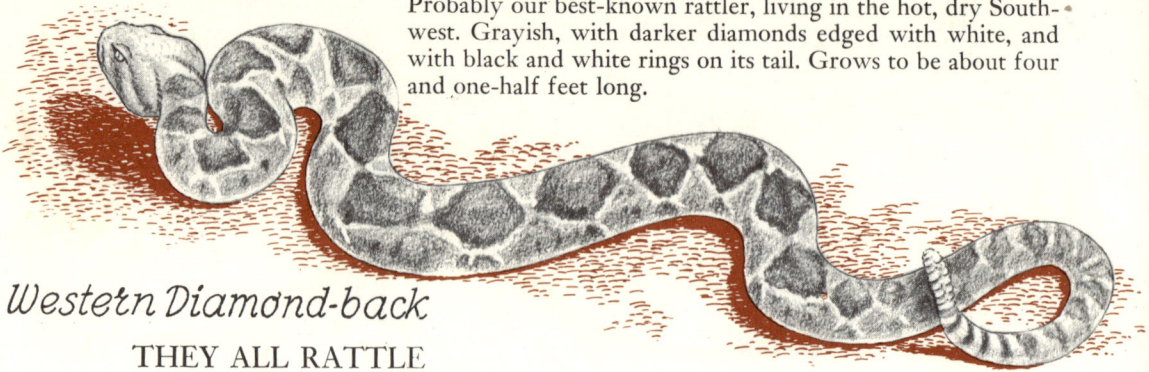

Western Diamond-back

THEY ALL RATTLE

We have more rattlesnakes in this country than any other poisonous snake—over fifteen species in all. All except some of the most northern states have at least one kind of rattler. Rattlesnakes are different in different parts of the country. Some are large, some are small, their markings are not all alike—but they all rattle.

Their rattles are interlocking sections at the ends of their tails. Each time a rattlesnake sheds its skin, a new rattle is left. This locks into the ones behind it. When the snakes get angry and shake their tails, these rattles-within-rattles click against each other. Rattles break off easily; most rattlesnakes do not have more than nine at one time.

The snakes pictured on these two pages are only a few of our rattlers. Be sure to find out if these are rattlesnakes in your part of the country. Then stay out of their way.

Our largest and deadliest poisonous snake, often growing to be six feet long. Lives in the wild brush country of the South. Olive-colored, and along its back are diamond-shaped mark-ings—dark with light borders.

Eastern Diamond-back

Prairie Rattlesnake

This snake lives in many places west of the Mississippi River—in flat grasslands, not rocky country. Often uses old prairie-dog burrows as dens. Grayish or greenish, with darker blotches. Sometimes five feet long.

Timber Rattlesnake

Lives in most eastern states, and west as far as Iowa and Texas, usually among rocks in woods. Color and markings vary—often they are yellow or brown with wavy dark crossbands. Also called the banded rattlesnake.

Pigmy Rattlesnake

Only about eighteen inches long, the smallest rattler east of the Rockies. Ashy gray with black blotches. Lives in dry sandy places or pine woods in the South, and westward to Texas and Oklahoma.

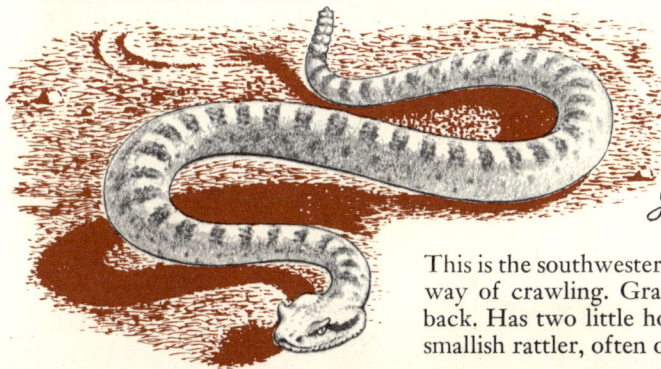

Sidewinder

This is the southwestern desert snake with the strange, sidewise way of crawling. Gray or brown, with dark blotches on its back. Has two little horn-like growths, one over each eye. A smallish rattler, often only two feet.

RECOGNIZING POISONOUS SNAKES

It would be fine if there were one simple rule that would tell you all our poisonous snakes at a glance. But there isn't. Of course, they all have fangs—they're alike in that. But by the time you find that out, you may have been bitten.

Pit vipers—water moccasins, rattlesnakes and copperheads—have eyes with vertical pupils, like a cat's in daytime. But several harmless snakes do, too. And anyway, it's hard to see eyes without getting up too close for comfort.

But here are some STOP, LOOK, AND LISTEN rules to remember before going too near a snake:

1. *All* rattlesnakes have *rattles* at the ends of their tails. Even the babies have one little button there. If they are taken by surprise, rattlesnakes sometimes strike without rattling. But you usually hear their warning whir first.

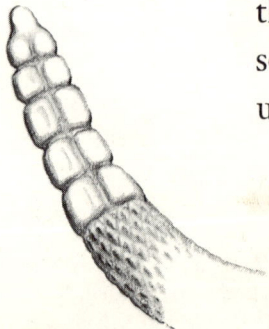

44

2. Water moccasins, copperheads and rattle-snakes have *pits* in their snouts, in addition to their nostrils.

3. Water moccasins, copperheads and rattle-snakes have *wide, triangular-shaped heads* on thin necks. Some harmless snakes do, too. But look twice before going too near snakes with heads like this. And if in doubt, stay away.

4. Coral snakes have rings going all around their bodies in this arrangement of colors: red, yellow, black, yellow—red, yellow, black, yellow. The yellow rings are narrow. Several other snakes, like the scarlet snake and the scarlet king snake, are "mimics" of the coral snake —they all look much alike. But remember: The coral snake is the *only* red, yellow and black ringed snake that has the red ring next to the yellow. *Red and yellow rings touching*—that is the "keep-away" sign!

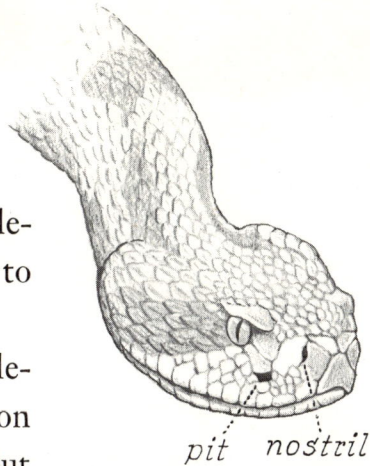

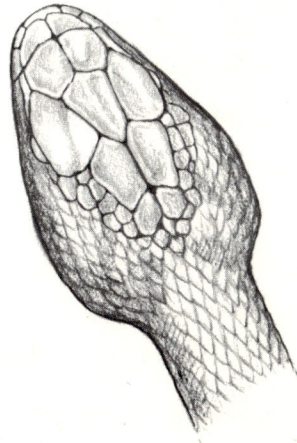

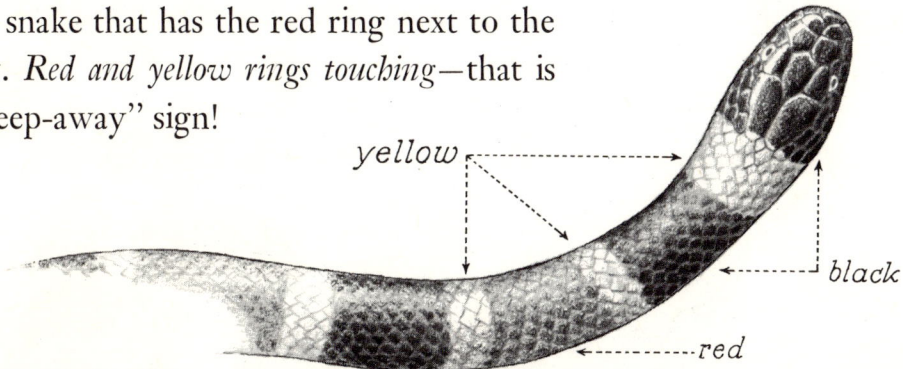

pit   nostril

yellow

black

red

ABOUT SNAKE POISONING

Poisonous snakes are as dangerous as live high-tension electric wires. Let them strictly alone. Only a snake expert should handle *any* poisonous snake. If you go where poisonous snakes are known to be abundant, wear heavy boots, or heavy leggings and leather shoes. Wear heavy leather gloves when climbing up ledges. Remember that a snake may strike when frightened or surprised.

Many non-poisonous snakes bite, too, if they are annoyed. Their teeth leave a line of scratches which may become infected if not cared for. Painting with iodine may be all the care that these non-poisonous snake bites need. Poisonous snakes have two long fangs. They sink their fangs deep, and leave one or two real holes that look very different from tooth scratches. They need first-aid treatment.

If, by chance, you or your companion is bitten, apply a tourniquet above the wound at once. Then, if possible, phone a doctor and do what he says. Don't let the victim move quickly. That starts the poison circulating through his body. If possible, carry him limp or on a litter. Following is the way to treat poisonous snake bite. Always have a grownup do this when possible. If you have to do it, be careful not to cut the victim harmfully.

46

1. Tie a necktie, handkerchief, belt or piece of cloth about two inches above the bite. Don't tie it too tightly—just enough so that you can squeeze a finger between it and the skin. Every fifteen minutes, loosen this tourniquet for one minute, to allow the blood to circulate a little, but not enough so that the poison gets carried all through the blood stream.

2. Quickly sterilize a knife blade or razor blade (use a match flame if you have no antiseptic). Make an X-shaped cut, at least a quarter of an inch long and a quarter of an inch deep, over each fang mark.

3. Suck out the blood and venom from the cuts. You can suck with your mouth and spit out the venom, unless you have cuts in your mouth or on your lips. Venom is dangerous only if it gets into your blood stream, and it can do this only through an open cut. If you spend much time in country where there are poisonous snakes, you would best buy a snake bite first-aid kit at a sports goods shop or a drug store, and have it with you on hikes. These kits have rubber suction bulbs to use for sucking out venom.

4. Make new cuts as the wound keeps swelling, and keep on sucking. Keep moving the tourniquet above the swelling.

5. Get the patient to a doctor as fast as possible. But do not let him run. Keep him as quiet as possible.

The doctor will give the patient an injection of serum called anti-venin. Right away this starts acting against the snake venom that is still in the patient's blood stream.

Anti-venin is made by injecting small, then larger, doses of snake venom into horses until they become immune to it. Then a serum is made from the blood of these horses.

Poisonous snakes are kept on snake farms just to furnish the snake venom that helps in making anti-venin. Every once in a while the snakes are "milked" of their poison. That is, their heads are held over a glass container while the venom is gently squeezed out of their poison glands down through their fangs. So, some poisonous snakes help to remedy the harm that others do. Anti-venin has saved many human lives.

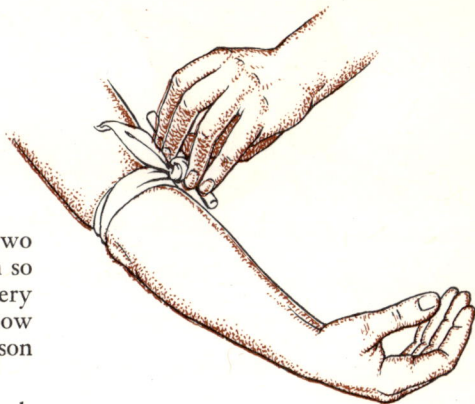

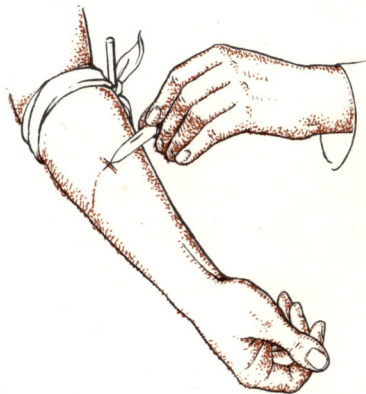

47

SNAKES LIVE IN MANY PLACES

There are over two thousand kinds of snakes in the world, ranging from the tiny worm snakes that are only about six inches long to pythons that grow to over thirty feet. Snakes are almost everywhere on earth except in really cold places and on some islands.

They have changed in many different ways so that they are fitted to their special homes. This gives them great variety. A few desert snakes have gradually grown to have colors that match their surroundings. They have become burrowers. Some of them can sink out of sight, in the sand, quick as a flash. Other desert snakes can actually crawl around, completely covered, beneath the sand.

Sea snakes have developed a tail shaped like an oar, that helps them swim. Tree snakes are good climbers. Other kinds of snakes have ways that particularly fit them to the places where they live.

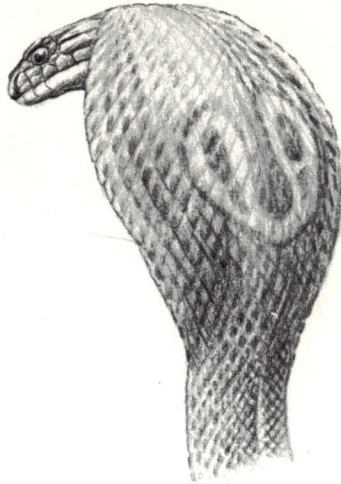

SOME ZOO SNAKES

A visit to the zoo will give you an idea of how very different snakes can be.

The poisonous cobras are interesting. They raise their heads and spread their hoods when they are angry, then strike with a swatting downward motion. They live in Africa, Asia, and the Philippine Islands. The king cobra is the world's largest poisonous snake. It eats other snakes almost entirely, for food. The spectacled cobra of India has markings like eyeglasses on the back of its hood.

The gaboon viper is a strange-looking snake from Africa, colored brown and buff and purplish in a very complicated pattern. It is short and strong and stout, with a big wide head and two enlarged scales on its snout. Its long and powerful fangs carry a deadly poison. Gaboon vipers are altogether unpleasant creatures, but fascinating to look at.

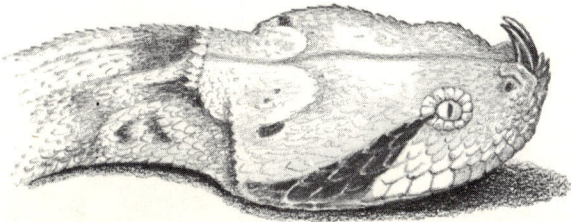

Tree snakes are some of the most fascinating ones. They live in trees and travel from branch to branch, straightening themselves as stiff as a wire as they reach out, and gradually uncurling themselves from one branch as they go to another. You can hardly believe how easily they move about above the ground. When they are resting, some of them spread at full length along a branch. Others curl up on it, arranging their coils to drop down on either side so that they are perfectly balanced. The green tree boa, a South American snake, is bright green with little white markings on its back that look as if they had been daubed on with a paint brush. The Asian long-nosed tree snake has a long, narrow head. You may see these and others at the zoo. Tree snakes eat lizards, and birds and their eggs.

Water Snakes

Water snakes are often found in wooded places, although they are not climbers. They spend a great deal of time in the water, looking for food. But often they lie along branches overhanging ponds and streams. When danger threatens, they drop down and swim away.

One of the odd water snakes of other countries is the dog-faced water snake of India and Malay and some of the Pacific Islands. It has a big jaw that makes its face look a little bit like a dog's. This snake sometimes hitches its tail around a piece of branch that is underwater. Then it waits quietly, to grab the first unsuspecting fish that swims by.

Common water snakes are plentiful in this country. They are ugly-looking and chunky, with wide heads something like pit vipers', though they are not poisonous.

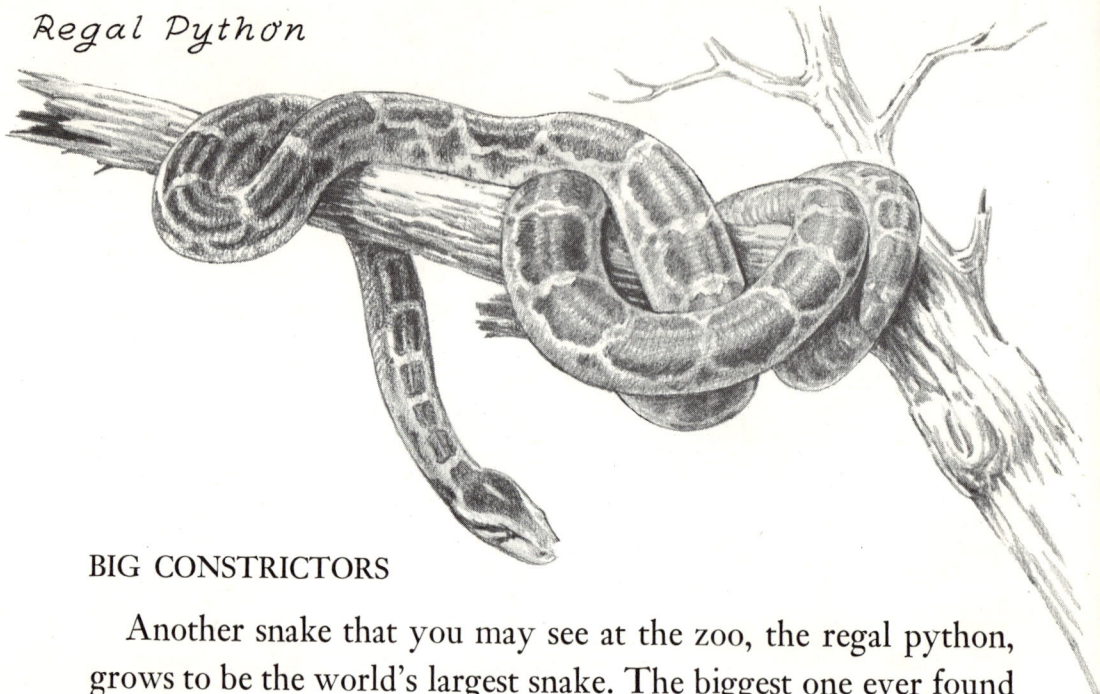

BIG CONSTRICTORS

Another snake that you may see at the zoo, the regal python, grows to be the world's largest snake. The biggest one ever found was thirty-three feet long. Regal pythons have markings of light and dark brown, and yellow. They are quite slender. A twenty-five foot python is eight or ten inches around and weighs about 250 pounds. Pythons come from Asia and the Philippine Islands. In the jungle they feed on small deer, wild pigs, jackals, birds, and snakes, which they kill by constriction. They are not poisonous.

Another big snake is the anaconda, a water snake of South America, which has black markings on its dark olive-colored skin. It does not grow as long as the python—twenty-eight feet is the longest known—but it is much stockier, as big around as a small barrel. Anacondas can eat animals weighing over one hundred pounds. They are constrictors, too.

52

Do you know these? ——

There are 126 species of snakes in the United States and some of these are divided into several varieties. So you can see that there are only a few poisonous snakes and many that are harmless. These are a few of the well-known harmless snakes:

De Kay's snake
Brown or gray, with a lighter streak down its back. Only about ten inches long. Very common east of the Rockies, in orchards, meadows, thickets, even in city parks. Eats earthworms, slugs and insect larvas.

Gopher snake
Gopher snakes live in the far West, where they eat gophers, rabbits, mice, ground squirrels and small birds. The Pacific gopher snake has dark blotches on a pale brown body. Bull and indigo snakes are sometimes called gopher snakes, too.

Milk snake
Gray or light brown, with black-edged, reddish-brown blotches on its back, and smaller spots on its sides. Often stays around barns, catching mice. Farmers used to believe it milked the cows, but that is not true.

53

and these ? —

Corn snake

Very handsome—light reddish-gray with bright red blotches rimmed with black. Grows from three to six feet. Catches mice that eat the corn when it is ripening. Also eats birds and their eggs, and small rabbits.

Pine snake

Has dark blotches on a dull white or pale gray background. Grows to about five feet. Usually lives among pine trees. Eats mice, rats, squirrels, birds and their eggs.

Slender, plain black. Grows to about four feet. Eats mice, frogs, other snakes, lizards, birds and their eggs.

Black snake

Pilot Blacksnake

Bigger and shinier than common black-snakes, and with ridged scales. Often grows to five or six feet. Eats squirrels, mice, frogs, lizards, birds and other snakes.

Garter snake

Has three pale yellowish stripes against a dark background. Sometimes two feet long. Eats earthworms, salamanders, toads, frogs. One of the best-known snakes.

Whip snake

Long, slender whip snakes live in many places. They eat insects, birds and small animals. The California striped whip snake has light yellow stripes on a dark body.

or these ? ——

King snake

Black, with a white, chain-like pattern. Grows to about three and one-half feet. Eats frogs, lizards, small animals and other snakes, even poisonous ones. Gentle, as a pet.

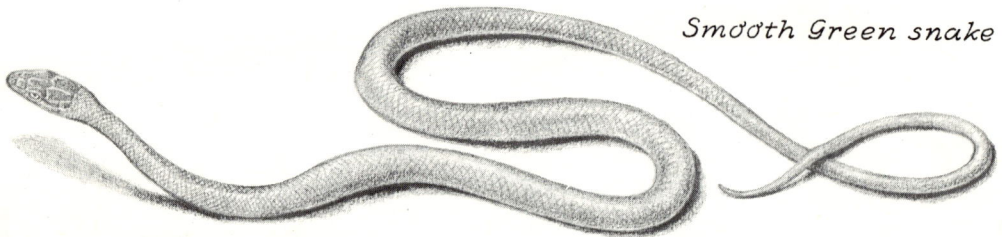

Smooth Green snake

Light green and slender. Grows to about fifteen inches. Lives in moist green meadows where it catches crickets, grasshoppers and other insects for food. A gentle pet.

Rough Green snake

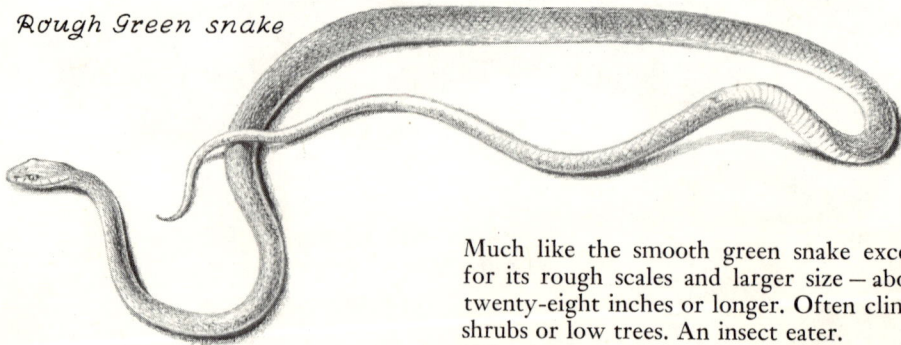

Much like the smooth green snake except for its rough scales and larger size — about twenty-eight inches or longer. Often climbs shrubs or low trees. An insect eater.

Patchnosed snake

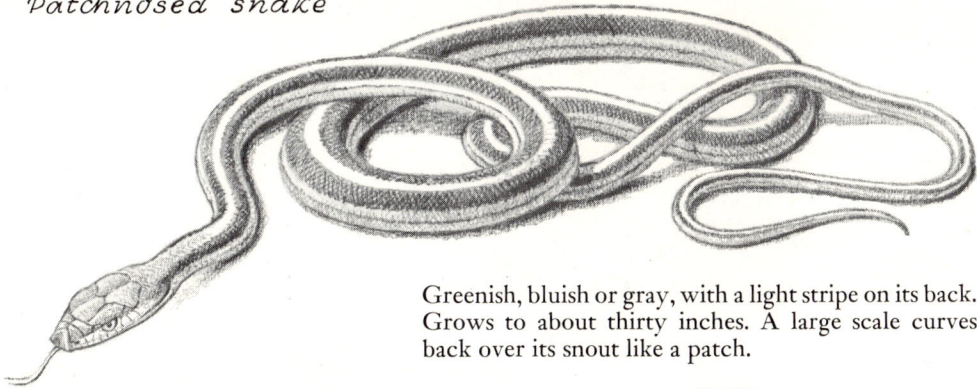

Greenish, bluish or gray, with a light stripe on its back. Grows to about thirty inches. A large scale curves back over its snout like a patch.

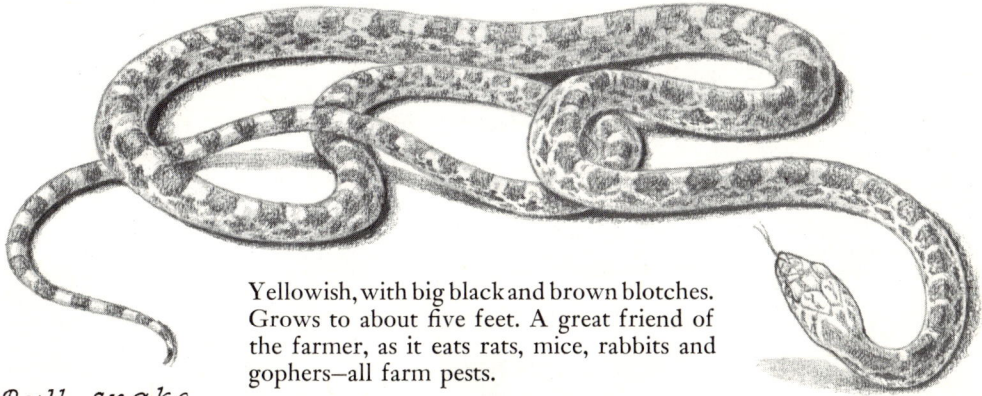

Yellowish, with big black and brown blotches. Grows to about five feet. A great friend of the farmer, as it eats rats, mice, rabbits and gophers—all farm pests.

Bull snake

Striped—looks a little like a garter snake, though its slender body is more ribbony. Grows to about two feet. Lives near water and eats frogs, salamanders, tadpoles.

Ribbon snake

SNAKES AS PETS

You may wish to keep a few snakes at home. By watching, you will soon learn where to find them. Always collect the snakes from your part of the country. Then if you have to let them go after a while, they can survive.

Before you start snake-hunting, find out the poisonous snakes in your vicinity, what they look like, and where they usually are. And don't try to collect them. If you have to look for snakes near where there are poisonous ones, wear high-top boots, or leggings over leather shoes. If you climb among rocks, wear heavy leather gloves. Don't move rocks or logs with your hands. Use a metal poker.

In very early spring, you can find snakes near their dens. In summer, look in cool, moist places. Try looking under small rocks, logs, and loose bark on trees. Pieces of wood on the ground may hide snakes, too.

To catch a harmless snake, come up to it slowly from behind, then grab it quickly behind its head. It may thrash around, but hang on firmly. Pick it up gently when it quiets down. Don't let it dangle from its head or tail. Rest its body in your other hand. Cloth sacks tied around with cord are good for carrying snakes. For small snakes, you can use screw-top jars. Make the air holes from the inside of the covers, to keep the inside surface smooth. Keep sacks and jars out of the sun when they have snakes in them.

The best kind of snake cage is of wood, with a glass front. For small snakes like DeKay's, a cage 12x8x8 inches is big enough. For snakes two feet long, one 26x18x16 inches is good. Have the cage long enough for the snake to stretch out in. Fasten the glass onto the front with strips of wood. Hinge the lid, and put a good hook on it. Drill plenty of air holes, all smaller than the snake's head, at each end of the cage. Don't use screens, as snakes rub on them and cut themselves. Put enough varnish on the floor inside so that the wood will not absorb moisture.

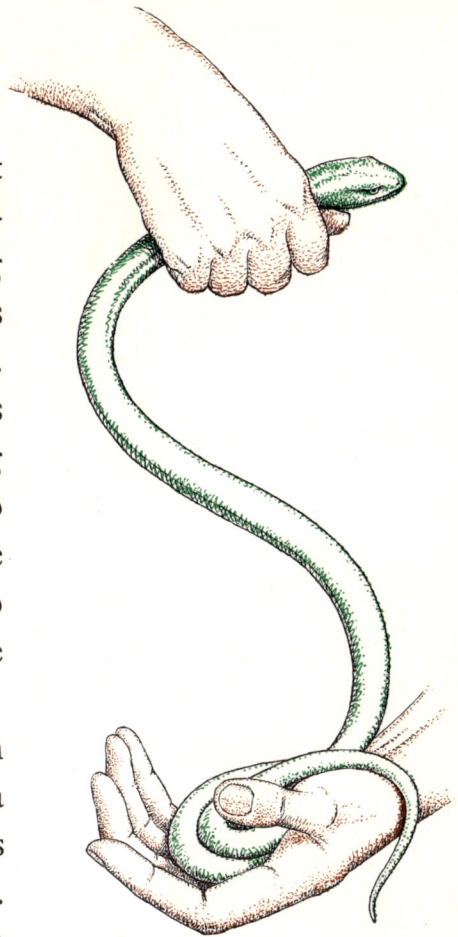

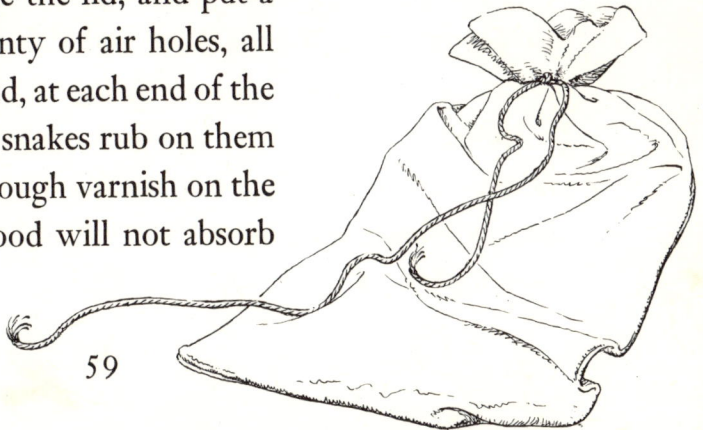

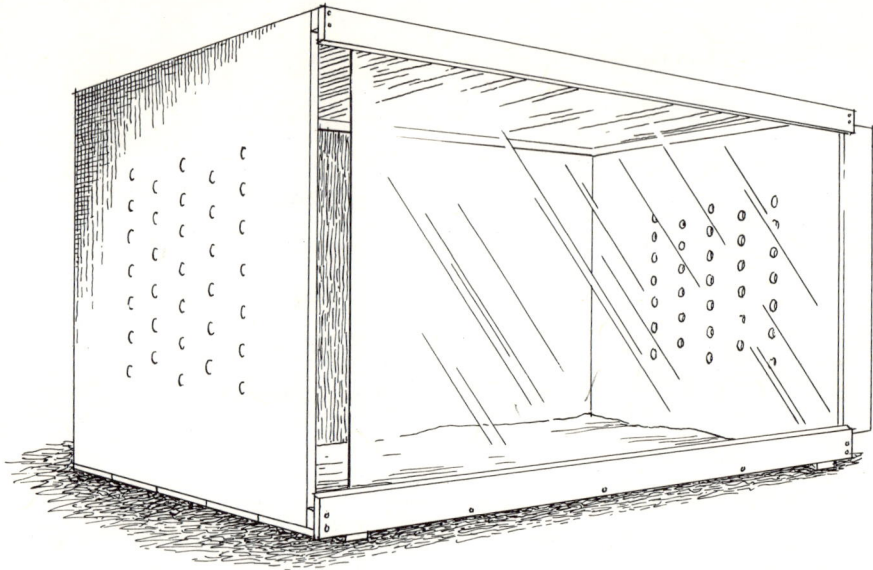

Several layers of newspaper on the floor of the cage make cleaning easy. Change them for fresh ones whenever necessary. A heavy glass or crockery water dish in one corner is important. So is something for the snake to crawl under. This can be a piece of bark lifted off the floor by strips of wood. Snakes that climb like a piece of tree limb, or a rod across the cage. A rock is good, too, for snakes to rub against while shedding their skins.

Keep the cage out of the sun and in a fairly even temperature— between 65 and 80 degrees. Snakes will not hibernate if the temperature is warm. But finding food for them in winter is often hard, so you may want to let them go in early fall, and catch new ones in the spring.

A cage for each snake is best. In any case, keep each snake alone while you are feeding it. Otherwise, if two snakes take hold of the same piece of food, one may disappear down the other's throat. And remember, don't put king snakes and other snake-eating varieties in cages with other snakes.

Getting food for your snakes and getting them to eat it is often your biggest problem at any time of year. If a snake won't eat, leave its food in the cage overnight. If the food is still there in the morning, take it out and try again in a day or two. When a snake will not eat by itself, it is best to let it go, and catch another that is a better eater. Zoos sometimes have a method of forcing snakes to eat. But it is difficult, and often is not good for the snake. So it is best not to try it with your snakes.

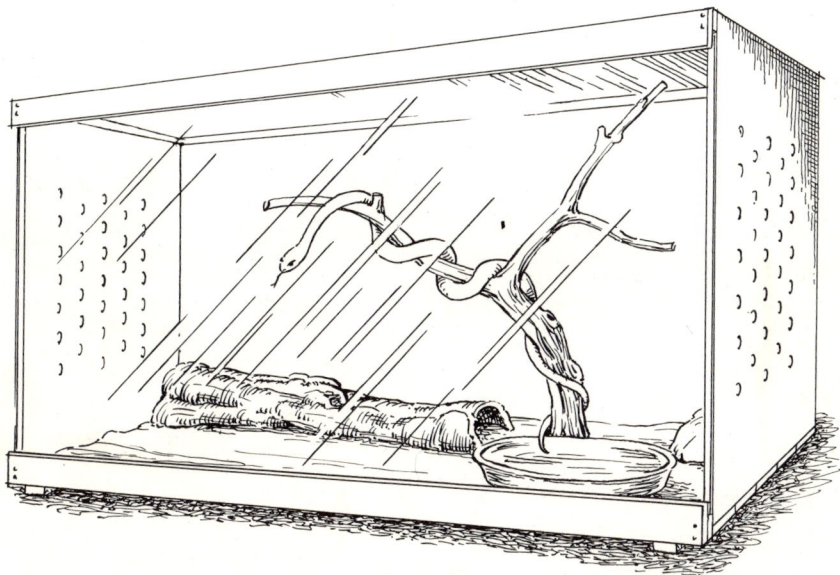

You will soon learn what your snakes like to eat, and where you can find it. Here are a few snakes that make good pets—this is the food they like: DeKay's snakes like slugs, insects, worms, grubs; ribbon snakes like salamanders, small frogs; garter snakes like earthworms, small frogs, toads, salamanders; green snakes like caterpillars, insects; king snakes like small snakes, lizards, mice, frogs, small eggs; corn snakes like mice. After you have had your snakes awhile, you may train them to eat chopped meat or fish. A good-sized meal once a week is enough for a snake. That is a meal that makes a real bulge in its body.

You may be lucky enough to find some snake's eggs, or one of your snakes may lay some. And of course you will want to try hatching them. Put some moist paper towels in a flower pot or crock, and place the eggs on top of them. Cover the flower pot or crock with a piece of glass, and place it in a warm spot, not over 95 degrees. Be sure to keep the towels damp, but not wet. After some time, the eggs may look bumpy in spots. If so, they are getting ready to hatch. Keep watching, and try to see the baby snakes coming out of the eggs.

Always treat your snakes kindly. Keep their cages clean and at a temperature they like, 65 to 80 degrees. Give them fresh water every day. Handle them gently. Don't tease them. Approach them slowly, without startling them. Even if they are jumpy at first, almost all of them will calm down and become quite tame if they are well treated.

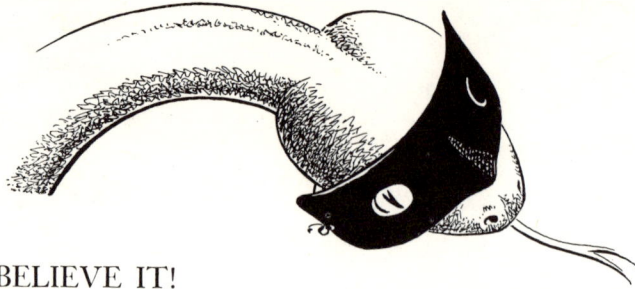

DON'T BELIEVE IT!

The more you watch snakes the more interesting they will become. You will keep finding out new things about them. And you may find that some of the old things you learned before are not true. For people have believed many strange things about snakes, and have told them as true stories.

Here are a few of the myths about snakes—with the real truths:
Myth: A milk snake robs cows of their milk. *Truth:* A milk snake could not reach a cow to milk her. (And a milk snake has very sharp teeth. It couldn't milk a cow without biting her badly. No cow would put up with that!)
Myth: Snakes are slimy. *Truth:* They have very dry, very clean skins. Even when they have been in water, they dry quickly.
Myth: Snakes sting with their tongues. *Truth:* Their tongues carry particles to the smelling organs in their mouths.
Myth: A mother snake swallows her young to protect them from enemies. *Truth:* If she did, her strong digestive juices would certainly finish off the young snakes. Someone may once have killed a mother snake that was about to give birth to live baby snakes. Not knowing that some snakes do this instead of laying eggs, this person may have thought she had swallowed the little snakes.

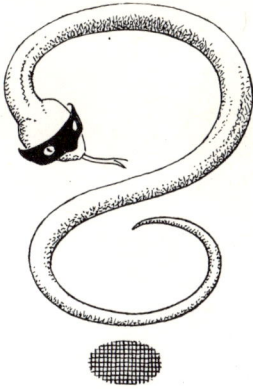

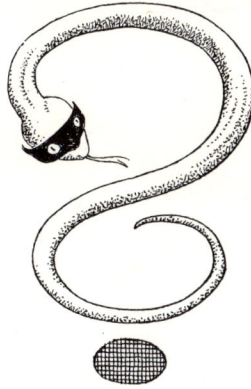

Myth: There is a hoop snake that can take its tail in its mouth and roll along like a hoop, chasing people. The tip of its tail is also a deadly sting. *Truth:* No snake can make itself into a rolling hoop. There is a southern mud snake that has a sharp spine on the end of its tail, but it is not poisonous.

Myth: Snakes can charm their prey by staring at them. *Truth:* Snakes do stare, because they have no movable eyelids, and cannot wink. And sometimes their prey are caught because they crouch quietly, as if they were hypnotized. But the victims stay still because many times before they have escaped attention in this way. The snake has not charmed them.

Myth: A snake that has been killed does not really die until sundown. *Truth:* Snakes die when you first kill them. But they may continue to move a little because some of their muscles flex for a while even after they are dead.

Myth: A rattlesnake will not crawl over a horsehair rope. *Truth:* It will crawl over a horsehair rope as readily as it will crawl over the ground itself.

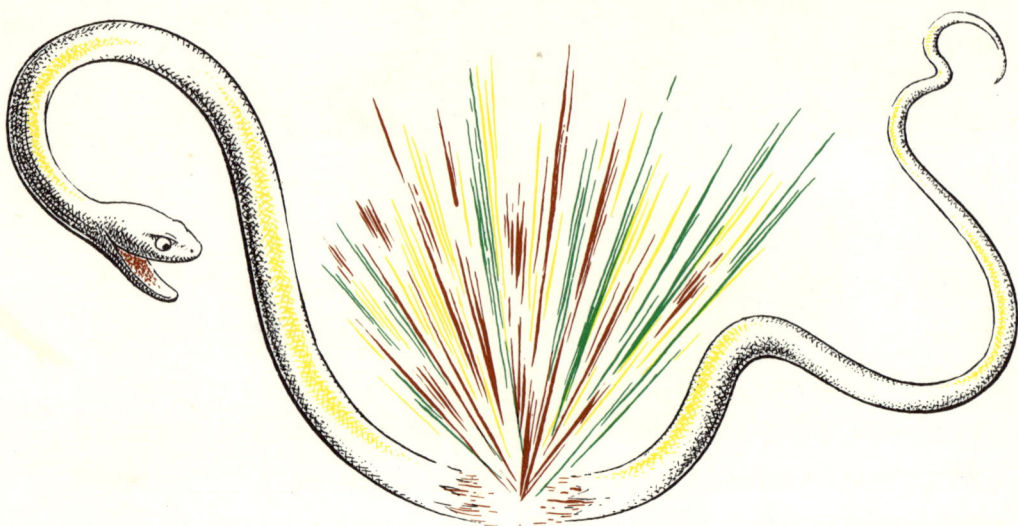

Myth: You can tell a rattlesnake's age by the number of its rattles. *Truth:* A rattlesnake's rattles break off easily. Probably few rattlers go through life keeping a complete set. The very first rattle a snake ever gets is like a little bulb. If the snake has that at the tip of its tail, it has not lost any rattles. You cannot tell its age, though. Snakes vary in the number of rattles they get each year.

Myth: There is a snake that flies apart if you strike it. Later, when you are gone, it puts itself together again. *Truth:* There is a long-tailed, legless lizard that looks like a snake. (But its jaws are not divided in front, like a snake's. And it has movable eyelids.) This lizard—the glass snake is its name—has a tail that breaks off when it is seized. The lizard escapes, and grows a new tail after a while. No snake can break its tail off, and not even a lizard can put its old one back on again.

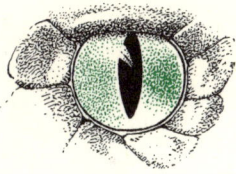

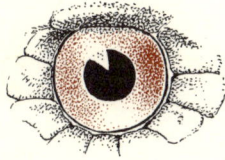

Myth: The coachwhip snake will lash a person or animal to death. *Truth:* This would be an impossible performance for any snake.

Myth: Snakes that have eyes with vertical, cat-like pupils are poisonous. *Truth:* The pit vipers have eyes like this, but some harmless snakes do, too. And poisonous coral snakes have eyes with round pupils.

Myth: You can tell a poisonous snake by its wide, triangular-shaped head. *Truth:* The pit vipers have heads like this, but so do some harmless snakes. And the coral snakes have round heads about the same width as their bodies.

Myth: Constrictors break every bone in their victims' bodies before starting to swallow them. *Truth:* Constrictors squeeze their victims only hard enough to stop their breathing, and possibly to stop their hearts' beating.

Myth: You can make a poisonous snake harmless by taking out its fangs. *Truth:* Snakes have a *pair* of fang sockets in each upper jaw. Before an old fang drops out, a new one has appeared alongside it, to take its place. Sometimes the old and the new fang may both be working.

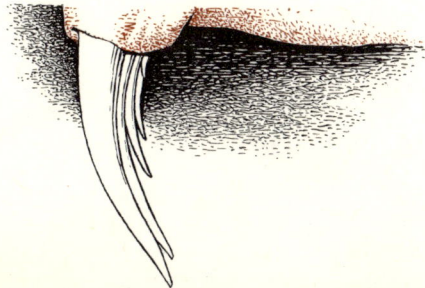

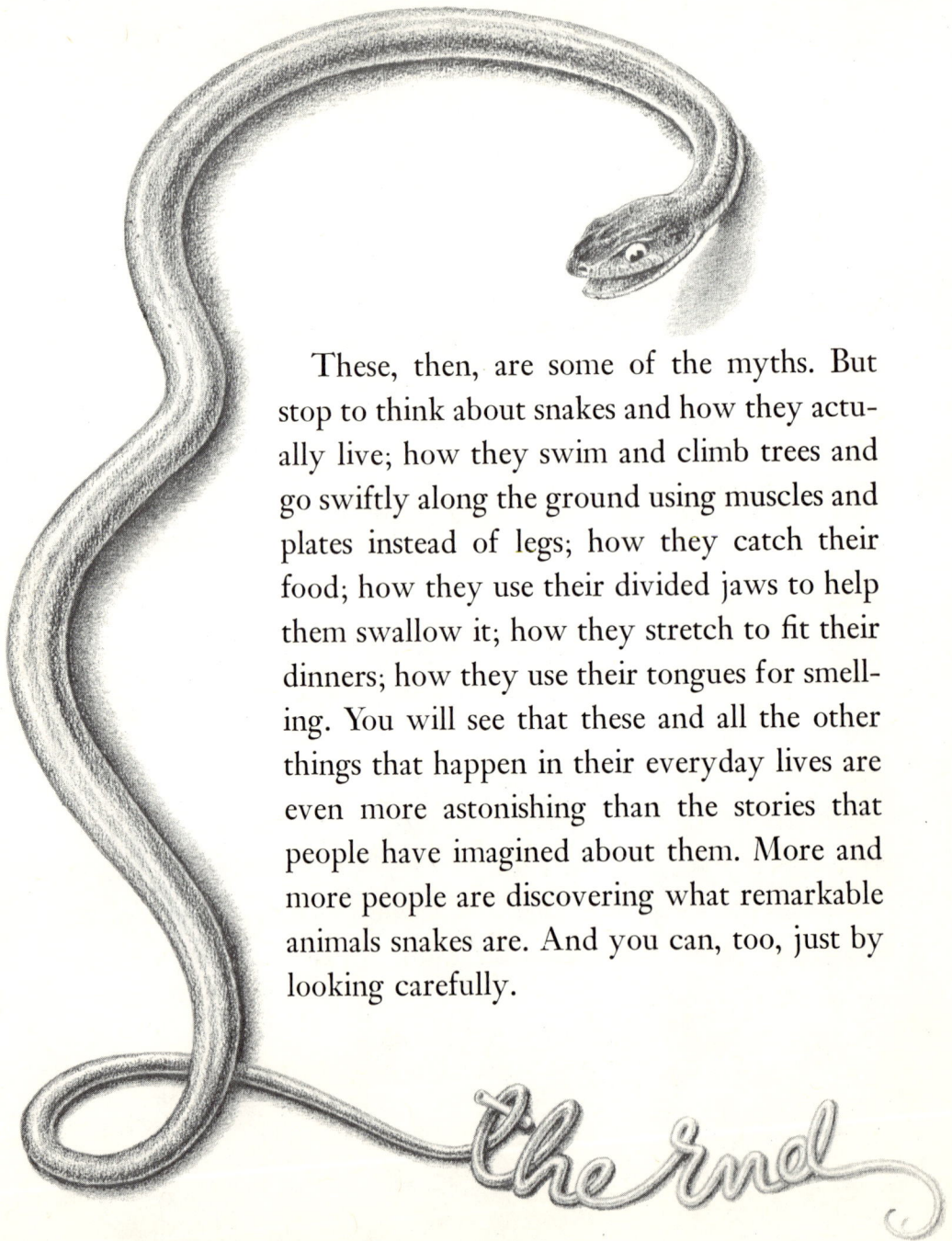

These, then, are some of the myths. But stop to think about snakes and how they actually live; how they swim and climb trees and go swiftly along the ground using muscles and plates instead of legs; how they catch their food; how they use their divided jaws to help them swallow it; how they stretch to fit their dinners; how they use their tongues for smelling. You will see that these and all the other things that happen in their everyday lives are even more astonishing than the stories that people have imagined about them. More and more people are discovering what remarkable animals snakes are. And you can, too, just by looking carefully.

the end

INDEX

Anaconda, 52
Anti-venin, 47
Backbone, 15
Birth, 31-32
Black snake, 54
Bluffing, 35-37
Body temperature, 28
Bull snake, 57
Catching, 59
Cobra, 37, 49
Collecting snakes, 58-59
Constrictors, 21, 52, 67
Copperheads, 35, 38-39, 44-45
Coral snakes, 38, 41, 45
Corn snake, 32, 54, 62
Courtship, 30
Crawling, 15-17
DeKay's snake, 53, 62
Desert snakes, 17, 48
Digestion, 27
Dog-faced water snake, 51
Drinking, 27
Eating, 19, 23-27
Egg-eating, 27
Egg tooth, 32, 33
Eggs, 31-32, 63
Enemies, 35-37
Eyes, 18, 33-34, 44, 67
Fangs, 21-22, 24-25, 67
Fighting, 35-37

Food, 19, 62
Gaboon viper, 49
Garter snake, 23, 31, 55, 62
Gopher snake, 53
Green snake, 56, 62
Green tree boa, 50
Hatching, 32, 63
Heads, 45, 67
Hearing, 18
Hibernation, 28-29
Jaws, 24-26
King snake, 56, 62
Long-nosed tree snake, 50
Mating, 29-30
Milk snake, 53, 64
Milking venom, 47
Moccasin, 38, 40, 44-45
Mouths, 24-26
Muscles, 15-17, 26
Myths, 64-67
Nests, 31-32
Patchnosed snake, 57
Pet snakes, 58-63
Pilot black snake, 55
Pine snake, 54
Pit vipers, 38, 41, 45
Plates, 15-16
Poisonous snakes, 38-47
Python, 48, 52
Rattlesnake, 31, 38, 42-45, 65-66

Rear-fanged snakes, 22
Ribbon snake, 57, 62
Ribs, 15
Rough green snake, 56
Scales, 14, 26, 35
Sea snakes, 48
Sidewinding, 17, 43
Skin, 26, 33-34
Skin shedding, 33-34
Smelling, 18-19
Smooth green snake, 56
Snake poison, 21-22, 47
Snake poisoning, 46-47
Stomach, 14, 26-27
Striking, 20
Teeth, 20, 24-25
Tongue, 18-19, 64
Tracks, 16-17
Tree snake, 35, 48, 50
Venom, 21-22, 47
Vipers, 22, 38, 41, 44
Water moccasins, 38, 40, 44-45
Water snakes, 19, 51
Whip snake, 55, 67
Windpipe, 26
Worm snake, 32, 48
Young snakes, 31-33
Zoo snakes, 49, 52